How to Make Decisions That Stay Made

D1291321

Jon Saphier
Tom Bigda-Peyton
Geoff Pierson

Association for Supervision and Curriculum Development
Alexandria, Virginia

Copyright © 1989 by Jon Saphier,
Tom Bigda-Peyton, and Geoff Pierson.

Printed in the United States of America.
Composition and printing by Automated
Graphic Systems.

ASCD publications present a variety of
viewpoints. The views expressed or implied in
this publication should not be interpreted as
official positions of the Association.

Ronald S. Brandt, *Executive Editor*
Nancy Carter Modrak, *Managing Editor, Books*
René M. Townsley, *Associate Editor*
Janet Price, *Assistant Manager, Production Services*
Cover design by Al Way, *Manager, Design Services*

ASCD Stock No.: 611-89132
ISBN: 0-87120-163-1

Cataloging-In-Publication Data:

Saphier, Jon.
How to make decisions that stay made.

1. School management and organization—United States—Decision
making. I. Bigda-Peyton, Tom. II. Pierson, Geoff. III. Title.
LB2806.S327   1989   371.2′07   89-15082
ISBN 0-87120-163-1

How to Make Decisions That Stay Made

Foreword   v

Why Must We Improve
Decision Making?   1

A Case Study in Decision Making   9

Overcoming Factors That Can Impede
Even a Good Decision-Making Process   30

Uses of the Decision-Making Guidelines   35

Conclusion   39

About the Authors   42

WITHDRAWN

Foreword

HOW TO MAKE DECISIONS THAT STAY MADE is a timely publication. Educators, in the United States and throughout the world, are looking for new structures to embue teachers with decision-making authority and responsibility. Authors Saphier, Bigda-Peyton, and Pierson agree that new structures may, indeed, be needed and certainly that decision making is a central issue. But they also argue against "throwing the baby out with the bath water." Before changing existing structures, they warn, we need to examine and improve our decision-making processes.

This slim little volume offers a dozen guidelines for the kind of successful decision making that not only leads to decisions that stay made but contributes as well to the organizational health of the school (or department or district . . .).

These 12 guidelines, or steps, are divided among three stages: planning, deciding, and implementing. While the labels are fairly traditional, recent thinking in organizational theory on group processes is reflected in this book. The guidelines constitute a framework for decision making that the authors advocate using prospectively and retrospectively. And, in a hypothetical scenario, they show us what dysfunctional decision making looks like and leads to and propose alternatives for effective decision making. Adherence to the guidelines, the authors promise, leads to improved organizational efficiency, effectiveness, and morale.

By teaching and modeling this decision-making process and making it public, the authors are helping us to carry out our ASCD mission, "Developing Leadership for Quality in Education for All Students."

PATRICIA C. CONRAN
President, 1989–90

Why Must We Improve Decision Making?

THE FOCUS OF THE '80S ON IMPROVING SCHOOLS and revitalizing the teaching profession has led to many proposals for changing the governance of schools (Rallis and Highsmith 1986, Darling-Hammond 1987). These proposals examine new structures for empowering teachers and giving them decision-making responsibilities over such issues as hiring, curriculum adoptions, teacher evaluation, and school policies. We believe that these proposals have identified the right issue, decision making, but have embarked prematurely on a course to generate new structures, roles, and governing bodies. There may well be a place for new structures of governance in schools, but before we abandon our current structures, we need to examine them to determine exactly what aspects of decision making are causing problems.

In our view, the process of legitimate decision making is neither well understood nor well implemented in most schools. This failure impedes effective school functioning, retards improvement, and makes teachers feel alienated. If the decision-making process were well understood and well practiced, teachers would feel more of the empowerment and efficacy that reformers are seeking. In short, *we must improve the process of decision making itself,* no matter what formal structures are invented to support it.

When decisions are viewed as legitimate, people feel appropriately involved and can therefore accept decisions, even those that are contrary to their personal views. Conversely, we have found that when a school or district has low morale or poor cohesiveness, decision-making processes are usually ailing. Often this inadequacy is at the root of the school's problems and needs to be addressed before we can expect commitment to school goals, collegiality among staff, or strength in any other norm of healthy school culture (Saphier and King 1985).

So it is important for school leaders to do everything possible to ensure that the decision-making process binds staff members together and leads to legitimate decisions. This is even more important in schools, in fact, than in other types of organizations (e.g., the military, corporations) where the chain of command and hierarchy of workers leave no doubt about which individuals have decision-making authority over others. Teachers function more autonomously than individuals in those other spheres. Policies, especially policies pertaining to instructional matters, often meet resistance if they arrive in classrooms without understanding and some degree of ownership by teachers, and they may be successfully sabotaged or ignored. Thus, leaders must pay particular attention to legitimate decision-making processes if they expect to enlist faculty in solving problems, changing instructional practices, or carrying out school improvement plans. A process for successful decision making not only produces better decisions, but builds the foundation for strong, healthy school cultures in every other respect.

A Typical Decision-Making Scenario

Consider this situation:

In his second year at Endicott High School, Principal Larry Burke announced at the first faculty meeting of the year the formation of a task group to study the 9th grade program and make recommendations for its improvement. He reported his sense from parents, middle school principals, and some school board members that there was some dissatisfaction with the program. He also mentioned that he had led a similar task group in his former assignment as assistant principal in another school.

Mr. Burke asked staff members to volunteer for the committee, the chairperson of which would be released from one class. Susan Freeman, an English teacher, was chosen to chair the group and immediately expanded it to include students and parents. In January the group reported to Mr. Burke and the faculty that they had divided into four subcommittees and were working on proposals to (1) improve students' transition from the middle school to high school, (2) create an advisor system, (3) personalize classroom and extracurricular activities, and (4) integrate academic disciplines.

At this point, a delegation of faculty informed Mr. Burke that they opposed the apparent directions of the task force and felt that Mrs. Freeman was addressing areas that were already working well. Mr. Burke said that he would have to reserve judgment until he had read the final report.

In late May, Mrs. Freeman presented her committee's report, which recommended the establishment of 9th grade advisors, workshops to train advisors, workshops to develop a writing program jointly taught by teams of social studies and English teachers, and the appointment of a freshman program coordinator who would teach a reduced load in order to plan transition activities before and during the 9th grade year. Because the school year was rapidly concluding, Mr. Burke thanked the committee and asked Mrs. Freeman to present the report to the school board during the summer. When the school board heard Mrs. Freeman at its July meeting, it praised the report and expressed the hope that the recommendations would be introduced soon.

The following November, Mr. Burke requested a meeting with Mrs. Freeman to discuss the status of the proposals. He told her that there was no money to support the committee's recommendations and that many faculty members had "legitimate concerns" about them. He planned to refer the proposals to the high school departments for discussion and reaction. Mrs. Freeman then called her committee together to announce, with a mixture of disappointment and anger, the status of their report.

In the short term, vocal dissatisfaction with the 9th grade program was reduced. The school board and the administration claimed that they were "working on" the problem, that the faculty had been involved in seeking solutions, and that only a tight budget was holding up improvements. The faculty remained divided over the nature and needs of the 9th grade program, however. Despite the attention given to the issue, the program remained unchanged.

We suspect that this case holds some genuine echoes of events readers have experienced. It is the all-too-frequent result of well-intentioned attempts at involvement winding up with most of the players feeling angry or disenfranchised. In this case it's even worse since no action is taken. We use this case in the next chapter as a springboard for exploring a new view of effective decision making in school organizations.

The Underpinnings of a Successful Process

In our view, effective decision making is a process that covers 12 bases, or steps, which, if successfully accomplished, will lead to legitimate decisions and, if regularly practiced, will build the foundation for a strong school organization. This process is based on our understanding of the distinctive nature of schools[1] and about what happens when these

---

[1] By distinctive, we mean that in schools that are "loosely coupled" (a term coined by Matthew Miles), many decisions are made, both in and outside of classrooms, that are not part of a central rational plan, nor are they implemented through commonly understood channels. Thus, the shape of what happens is much more dependent on individual personalities and informal communication patterns and is not explicable in terms of any organizational chart. For the most part, there *is* no formal organizational chart.

steps are *not* taken. It is also based on our belief that we must work hard to create conditions within organizations that encourage responsible participation—and that the progress of school depends on it.

A final underpinning of this process—and one that makes it different, we think, from others in the literature—is our emphasis on making it public. We advocate sharing and teaching the process to all members in the organization through modeling and explicit discussion. The goal should be for every member of the organization to be a responsible decision maker;[2] this goal is critical to school improvement. All of this implies that we do not do the process "to" or "on" people, nor is it a Machiavellian model for working one's will on others. It is, rather, a set of guidelines for making good decisions that will stay made.

Here are the 12 steps.

12 Steps for Making Successful Decisions

PLANNING

1. Identify and explicitly state the issue, who owns it, and what the underlying goal is.

2. Find out and explain how much discretion you have to take action or not. *Must* this issue be dealt with? State how strongly you personally feel about it.

3. Every issue lands in someone's lap to begin with. If it lands in yours, be sure to choose the proper path for who will make the

---

[2] We are indebted to Irwin Blumer and Carolee Matsumoto of the Concord Public Schools who brought this to our attention and who both model and articulate this value in their practice.

preliminary and the final decision, from
these options:

- An individual or group above you in
  the organization
- You as administrator unilaterally
- You as administrator with input from
  staff
- You as administrator and staff by
  consensus
- Staff, with input from you as
  administrator
- Staff by consensus
- Staff by vote
- Subgroup of staff, with input from
  others
- Subgroup of staff unilaterally
- Individual staff members unilaterally

4. At the beginning of the process,
   communicate clearly who will make the
   decision and identify any constraints that
   will affect the scope or content of the
   decision (i.e., staffing, budgeting, time).

5. State explicitly the values you want to
   maintain and why they are not negotiable if
   that is the case. (For example, "Whatever
   proposals come forward, I want to hang on
   to small class size and the high quality of
   personal student-teacher contact we get
   from that.")

DECIDING

6. Identify and periodically check out with
   people what the full impact or full
   consequences of the decision will be and
   communicate them to all parties involved.

7. Involve all parties whose working conditions will be affected by the decision.

8. Make clear the time line for deciding and implementing the decision.

9. Decide. Then make an explicit statement of the decision or recommendations, summarizing all key points.

10. Provide for exactly how and when the decision-making group will revisit the decision later to evaluate or revise it if necessary.

IMPLEMENTING

11. Close the loop. Communicate the reasons for the decision fully and clearly to all affected parties after the decision is made, including how people's input was used.

12. Plan how to monitor and support the day-to-day implementation of the decision and communicate these plans to everyone involved.

A Case Study in Decision Making

To Make the 12 Steps of Decision Making More meaningful, we expand on them in this chapter and apply each to the Endicott High School case presented in the previous chapter. How well did Principal Burke and other key players carry out those steps? What alternative actions might they have taken?

PLANNING

1. Identify the real issue.

   a. Explicitly state who owns it, who really cares about it, and why.

   b. Specify the underlying aim or goal to be attained.

In the Endicott High School situation, the statement of the issue was ambiguous. While Principal Burke told the faculty there was discontent with the 9th grade program, he did not specify the reasons for the dissatisfaction; as a result, the committee was left on its own to define the nature of the problem. This created the likelihood that the committee's function and authority would be widely misunderstood.

Had Mr. Burke held a discussion of the sources of discontent, he might have clarified the goals of the committee, identified potential opponents to the initiative early in the process, and considered whether their reservations made sense. For example, he could have stated some of the concerns and invited faculty reactions:

> As we plan for the coming year, I want to outline areas that require our collective attention. These have been identified by various individuals or groups. Let me list them. [Does so.] Have I left anything out?

> ... Given this list, I feel the 9th grade program is more important than other priorities, for these reasons. ... Does anyone see why we should place a higher priority on some of the other areas?

If the ensuing discussion produced a consensus that the dissatisfaction with the 9th grade program was ill-founded, Mr. Burke could have reconsidered the need for a committee. On the other hand, the discussion might have confirmed the need for the committee, identified different sides to the issue, and sharpened its focus. This kind of opening discussion would have helped the faculty understand the concerns that had been conveyed to Burke and, later on, to support necessary changes.[3]

2. *Find out and explain how much discretion you have to take action or not.* Must *this issue be dealt with? State how strongly you personally feel about it.*

   a. *Tell the decision-making group your thoughts about the answers to the above questions.*

   b. *If you have discretion, decide whether the issue is really worth working on now; e.g., does a decision really need to be made?*

      (1) *Examine your resources to see whether they're adequate for carrying out any solution (avoiding studies that are put on the shelf and waste people's time).*

      (2) *Verify that all the available data are accurate and complete.*

      (3) *Are there enough data to conclude there is a real problem or issue that is worth working on?*

---

[3] When initiating the decision-making process, it is extremely important to establish the expectation that communication will be open and honest. We talk more about this essential element on pages 30–31.

(4) *See whether the meaning of the data is significant enough to continue. Do others interpret the data the same way?*

(5) *How does this issue fit in with existing priorities? Will attention to this issue divert too many resources from other priorities?*

Mr. Burke did none of these things. As a result, the faculty had no sense of where this issue stood relative to other priorities of the school and school system. Again, this created the likelihood of misunderstandings later on, since people with different degrees of concern about the problem would have to address it without knowing whether the problem could be resolved in this particular year.

Alternatively, Mr. Burke could have charged the committee with exploring the problem and checking the completeness and accuracy of the data by interviewing those who had expressed concern about the 9th grade program. Mr. Burke could then have encouraged the committee to report their findings to the full faculty.

We also recommend Mr. Burke's informing the staff that this exploration of the problem will be done before deciding on *any* course of action, which includes the possibility that *no* action is needed, an option that should be included in the list of possible next steps after the committee's report. All too often when problems are raised for consideration, people automatically assume that the school or school system has committed itself to address them through some new program or initiative. This leads to the kind of overloaded agenda that can undermine the making of informed and effective decisions. Of course, if Mr. Burke believes that some action is necessary, he should say that at the outset, too, along with his rationale, and invite comment.

This step needs to be carefully considered whenever we approach a new problem, especially at the beginning of a school year when we tend to take on too many things. The issue here is whether there is enough *time*, a resource we often take for granted when pressed to work on new initiatives. If we do so without considering the impact on our ability to follow through, we sow the seeds for later frustration about our inability to adequately fulfill our stated objectives.

3. *Every issue lands in someone's lap to begin with. If it lands in yours, be sure to choose the proper path for who will make the preliminary and the final decision.*

    a. *Choose the appropriate path from among the following options:*

- *An individual or group above you in the organization*
- *You as administrator unilaterally*
- *You as administrator with input from staff*
- *You as administrator and staff by consensus*
- *Staff, with input from administrator*
- *Staff by consensus*
- *Staff by vote*
- *Subgroup of staff, with input from others*

- *Subgroup of staff unilaterally*
- *Individual staff members unilaterally*

b. *Test your decision about who will decide
in discussion with others who may lead
you to further insights.*

Mr. Burke missed this step at the outset. In
January, he said he would reserve judgment
until the final report, but even then he did not
explain to the faculty why he wanted to make
the decision this way and invite their
comments. This resulted in protests by faculty
later on that the committee was overstepping
its authority, since it was "addressing areas
that were already working well." Eventually,
Burke had to agree, acknowledging the
"legitimate concerns" of many faculty about
the recommendations eventually submitted by
the committee.

These problems could have been prevented
had Mr. Burke discussed with the faculty his
thinking about who would make the decision.
He could have said, "I plan to handle this by
making the decision myself after input from the
committee and you, and here's how I am
thinking of obtaining that input. . . . Any
comments on this?" This kind of statement
would have allowed him to test his views with
the faculty. He might have found that the issue
was going to affect more people than he had
realized. In that case, he might have recognized
that a consensus decision would be best since
most of the faculty would have to support it
actively for it to work.

In general, this step requires that Mr. Burke
think ahead to implementation while designing
a decision-making process. The more he needs

broad participation and ownership to be able to carry out possible changes, the more he should move toward a consensus method of deciding. And the only way he can establish this need is to explain his views about the process to the faculty and invite their reactions. There are usually several ways to make any decision, each of which might be valid for different reasons. What is important is not only that leaders make the "right" choice of decision path but that they share their thinking with others and invite discussion about that choice.

In this step, we envision Mr. Burke revisiting the issue of the 9th grade program in a full faculty meeting. This meeting constitutes a checkpoint—a way of underlining the need to engage faculty in determining an appropriate *process* for deciding before moving ahead on issues of *substance*. Here Burke should state his view of how and whether a decision should be made and test that view with everyone present. Let's say that Burke still thinks changes are needed in the 9th grade program but has changed his mind about going forward this year. He might say:

> The committee's inquiry into the concerns about the 9th grade program has reaffirmed my opinion that there are some problems we need to address. However, in the meantime, I've discovered that we probably won't have sufficient funds to pay for any recommendations we might want to implement. In addition, some other priorities have become more urgent than this one, for reasons I'll explain in a minute. So,

for now, I've decided not to proceed
with this initiative. However, I do
want to raise the issue so that you
can comment on the decision *not* to
work on this problem at this time.

Such a statement should separate the initial
investigation of a problem from a decision to
do something about it. It should give faculty an
opportunity to respond to the committee's
findings about the nature and severity of the
problem. The resulting discussion should lead
to increased commitment to doing something
about the problem, or at least should increase
understanding of what the committee is trying
to do.

It is important to note here, as elsewhere,
that leaders who conduct such a checkpoint
meeting must truly be open to new information
and to alternative ways of proceeding. If they
are not, they should not hold such a meeting,
or they should state the parameters of the
discussion, and the reasons for them, at the
outset. Otherwise, their efforts to involve
faculty appropriately in decision making may
be interpreted as another form of unilateral
control.

Finally, note how steps 2 and 3 come
together here in "real time." Although we've
broken out the steps separately for the sake of
emphasis and clarity, doing so in the stream of
events would often be artificial. In reality, clear
decision making will often simultaneously
address the questions "Do we have to act?"
and "Who will be the ultimate decision
maker?" The most important function of this
meeting is for Mr. Burke and the faculty to
decide whether to move ahead with some kind
of change in the 9th grade program. That

purpose will be served best if Mr. Burke summarizes his views on the need for a decision and the appropriate decision making path at the same time.

4. *At the beginning of the process, communicate clearly who will make the decision and identify any constraints that will affect the scope or content of the decision (i.e., staffing, budgeting, time).*

Once again, Mr. Burke did not observe this step. The result was that the committee later felt sabotaged when he said there was no money to pay for their proposals. Had he known this at the outset, he should have told them so that they and others could know the limits of their charter. More generally, when principals tell their faculty members whatever information they have about the likelihood of external support sooner rather than later, they prevent the experience shared by Mrs. Freeman and her committee members: working hard, then feeling undermined in the end.

5. *State explicitly the values you want to maintain and why they are not negotiable if that is the case. (For example, "Whatever proposals come forward, I want to hang on to small class size and the high quality of personal student-teacher contact we get from that.")*

This guideline involves pausing to reflect on strong values you want to see reflected in any solution that emerges.

Assume there has been sufficient agreement on the problem to justify the development of proposals to change the 9th grade program, that is, a decision to go ahead with the decision-making process (but not to go ahead with a plan since there is no plan yet). Burke may have a non-negotiable position about certain aspects of the current program that he wants to keep, regardless of any plan that will be developed. For example, he may want the school to retain the writing process approach in which he personally believes and in which the staff has invested three years of inservice work. He should tell this to the staff at this point in the decision-making process. *How* he states his position will make a difference, too.

If he said to the faculty, "I will not accept any change in 9th grade English," he would encourage less creative thinking than if he said, "At the moment, I can't see any acceptable way to change the way we teach writing, since we have an important schoolwide commitment to the process approach. However, I would be open to change in the English program if anyone can show me how the key elements of the writing process could be preserved." In the latter statement, he takes a firm stand but does not prevent further discussion. Even those who disagree with his stand can understand it if he explains his reasons. This understanding should increase the chances that staff will accept or at least not obstruct even those policies they oppose. In addition, this step will give people the feeling they have had a legitimate hearing in the course of policy formation.

In "real time," both steps 4 and 5 would probably take place in the same checkpoint faculty meeting in which Burke reviews the committee's initial investigation of the problem. These steps conclude the initial decision-making phase, planning, since they come after the faculty has decided to move forward with some kind of change but before the committee has developed and presented recommendations for discussion.

DECIDING

6. *Identify and periodically check out with people what the full impact or full consequences of the decision will be and communicate them to all parties involved.*

   a. *Sometimes communicating to everyone involves putting out a memo because there are more people involved than are around the table at the moment (or could fit around it at any moment).*

   b. *Examine long-term consequences of the decision in relation to the school's or district's overall goals.*

   c. *Examine the impact of the decision on school culture.*

Members of organizations often do not realize the full consequences of a pending decision. Thus they do not participate in the decision-making process even when asked; they wind up feeling aggrieved and later on complain that they didn't realize that "the administration had this in mind." Teachers who are busy with piles of papers to correct, a low-performing student or two that they're particularly worried about, and a wide range of students who may be challenging their ability to design lessons do not rush to join committees. They may also not listen well at a faculty meeting after school or thoroughly read a memo in their mailbox that describes concerns about the 9th grade program. It is important that faculty *do* listen well and *do* read memos when important issues are being considered. But given the quality of teachers' work lives, it is equally important for leaders who are guiding a decision-making process to be explicit and clear with people about the anticipated consequences of a decision.

In Burke's case, after preliminary discussions with the committee and after their presentations to the faculty, he might have said:

> Committing ourselves to a restructuring of the 9th grade program is likely to involve funding part-time positions of some kind. That is not a definite; our committee hasn't even entered the planning stage yet. But from my previous experience with projects of this nature, I'm pretty sure it would require additional spending for at least the first implementation year. Given our current budget policies, the school board is certain to instruct us to cover these expenditures from school-based funds. That means we won't have money for anything else new next year, and the permanent sub plan we've been hatching lately would have to take a back seat.

Here Burke would be alerting faculty to likely consequences of going ahead with the project at all—consequences for other programs they may have been counting on.

Now let's assume Burke had studied decision making *before* the 9th grade issue arose and handled everything beautifully through step 5 above. We might now imagine a faculty considering the committee's four recommendations with a well-developed sense of where the issue had come from and with a broad-based consensus that action should be taken. What they might not realize, however, is that the committee's third proposal, personalize classroom and extracurricular activities, has implications for all teachers who have 9th grade students, and that a substantial part of their inservice time next year will be committed to developing ways to implement those goals. If not Burke, then someone from the committee should explicitly surface the implications and communicate them to all concerned parties.

Failure to cover these bases leaves leaders open to charges that "You didn't tell me I would have to . . ." and "You didn't tell me this would take away my. . . ."

7. *Involve all parties whose working conditions will be affected by the decision.*

   a. *Be relentless in involving staff members but "protect what's important" by not involving them in trivial matters or matters they don't care or know much about.*

b. *Emphasize that anyone who chooses not to accept an invitation to participate in decision making has an obligation to accept the decision of others. Likewise, when participants sit at the table and don't speak, their silence means acceptance.*

c. *Having heard the concerns of relevant constituencies, take them into account and factor that into a decision about whether to scuttle the issue, reshape it, or continue.*

Since we have a goal to make everyone a responsible decision maker, it is important to reach out with information about pending decisions to all who may be affected, so they have an opportunity for input. This opportunity, however, should not be confused with the committee system run riot. Staff members neither need nor want to be involved in every decision. In fact, they may resent being asked to spend time on an advisory committee if the topic is one they know little about and the decision has little impact on them. A friend was recently asked to sit on a committee reviewing sabbatical proposals of fellow K-12 teachers and to recommend to the superintendent which ones to approve. As a high school guidance counselor, she didn't feel qualified to judge the importance to the school system of, for example, primary grade proposals to develop new reading materials or many other proposals before the committee. To be able to comment intelligently on many of the proposals would have required substantial reading and interviewing about the topics of the proposals.

This committee trap is sometimes sprung by an administrator who has fuzzy democratic feelings that "teachers should be involved" or who wants to be able to say teachers were involved in order to avoid criticism for being authoritarian. The fact is that staff members *want* administrators to make certain decisions because that is their job, and teachers, more than most, want their time for instructional planning and work with students protected against all but the most important encroachments.

In step 6 we made the point that administrators need to go out of their way to inform faculty about pending decisions and their consequences so that interested staff can participate if they want to. Now comes an important step in working to make everyone a responsible decision maker. Those who choose not to participate give up their right to complain later on. When informing staff members of meetings where decisions will be made or where input will be solicited for decisions to be made later, it is very valuable to say in writing, right in the memo, that *nonacceptance of the invitation to participate implies an obligation to go along with the decision the others make.* Likewise, when participants sit silently in meetings while decisions are being discussed, it is very valuable for the leader to reiterate that silence means acceptance of the decision (not necessarily enthusiastic endorsement, but at least a willingness to live with it and carry out one's part in implementing it faithfully). Both these moves encourage people to speak up honestly and own their views publicly. Often the group gets a new and important perspective from hearing the doubts of quiet members. At the other end of the spectrum, these moves directly confront the passive-aggressive behavior of members in an organization who say nothing and then resist or sabotage decisions later on. Such behavior is much less likely when members are held accountable for silence.

Burke never got anywhere near either or these steps (6 or 7) in the Endicott High School case. In another scenario, however, we might imagine the faculty, now committed to improving the 9th grade program, receiving an invitation to a meeting that would consider specifically the proposal for establishment of 9th grade advisors. This could be a voluntary meeting at which Burke explicitly reminds the participants that nonacceptance of the invitation to participate means an obligation to accept the decision others make.

8. Make clear the time line for deciding and implementing the decision.

Although Principal Burke apparently asked the Freeman committee to report by the end of the school year, he failed to impose any deadline or timetable for considering its recommendations. Having reviewed the committee's initial proposals at midyear, Mr. Burke might have determined whether Mrs. Freeman had "checked in" with other groups who might be concerned with the proposals. This supervision of the committee process is easy to neglect under the pressure of time.

In addition, at the final faculty meeting of the year Burke could have announced a schedule by which the recommendations of the Freeman committee would be reviewed in the coming academic year.

In cases such as these, we need to be aware that timetables may require adjustment as task groups encounter unanticipated complexities and the need to involve other people. We need to be alert to the possibilities that other priorities, which may appear later in the year, can threaten existing commitments and their time lines and make these conflicts known as they come up.

> 9. *Decide. Then make an explicit statement of the decision or the recommendations, summarizing all key points.*

This step may seem obvious, but it is often omitted. For reasons of simple clarity, leaders must ensure that such a statement appears, preferably in writing, for all to see. A decision should be identified and not confused with "current thoughts" or "proposals for your reactions," which may be circulated at numerous points during the decision-making process.

(It is equally important to label preliminary white papers and proposals as such; school staff members who are unused to careful decision making with genuine involvement have a tendency to believe that anything in writing is a decision even if you say it's not.)

> 10. *Provide for exactly how and when the decision-making group will revisit the decision later to evaluate or revise it if necessary.*

Again, Burke did not get this far. Had the school committed itself to creating an advisor system, however, now would be the time to set a date for the committee to evaluate the first year's implementation and recommend refinements or changes.

IMPLEMENTING

11. Close the loop. Communicate the reasons for the decision fully and clearly to all affected parties after the decision is made, including how people's input was used.

If representatives of a decision-making group are going to communicate the decision and its rationale to their constituencies, make sure they agree on how to frame it. They might practice or even role-play exactly what they will say to ensure they have a common understanding of what's been decided and why.

These steps accomplish several important things. First, if people have been asked for their advice, closing the loop makes them feel respected. When the ideas of a decision-making group are not reflected in the decision or its implementation plan, it's easy for group members to conclude—sometimes rightly, sometimes wrongly—that soliciting their ideas was a sham and the decision had already been made. It's even possible that the final plan could be the opposite of what they recommended. Under these circumstances, group members can understandably feel that their ideas were not valued and that they were "used." Their ideas, in fact, may have been carefully considered but ultimately rejected for good reasons. If they never hear what those reasons are, however, they might naturally assume the worst.

Informing people that their ideas were considered and *how* they were weighed against other ideas and constraints buys a sense of legitimacy for the decision. People can feel the process was fair and their views were really heard; they're more likely to go along with the decision even if they disagree with it. Without closing this loop, leaders are inviting passive resistance to the decision and, more generally, disaffection from their leadership itself.

A second consideration here is communicating *across echelons of the organization* how input was weighed and why the decision was made. At this point, we have been through all the weighing and balancing and now need to proceed with the plan. It is commonplace in high schools for this information to originate in a group of department chairpersons led by the principal and passed through each chair to faculty in department meetings. In parallel fashion, such information may pass from a superintendent's cabinet through principals to school faculties. And it is at this stage that much can go wrong.

For example, let us assume that in Mr. Burke's case, the decision-making process has moved to an advanced stage, and after much deliberation and faculty discussion, the decision is made to create an advisor system that gives each faculty member several advisees. The science department faculty has been opposed to an advisor plan since they're already overloaded with lab preparations and believe that the advisor system will dilute academic standards and content coverage in the school. They also oppose the diversion of next fall's inservice time from curriculum development to workshops and discussion groups on building productive advisor-advisee relationships.

Mrs. Lowe, the science chairperson, supports her department's position. But at this week's department chairs meeting with the principal, consensus has finally been reached to try the advisor system. What will she say at the next department meeting? How will she communicate the decision and what she expects of her department members in carrying it out?

This is the point at which the principal may want to go around the table and ask explicitly how chairs plan to communicate the decisions and their expectations to staff members. Mrs. Lowe has represented her department's position at previous meetings, but now that the decision has been made to introduce an advisor system she can be expected to work faithfully to try it out fairly and press her department members to do the same. Burke can legitimately expect Lowe to say something like this to her staff members:

> ... the bottom line is that we lost this one, and after a fair hearing of our views, the school is committed to trying the advisor system. So it is our obligation during the pilot year to give it our best shot and implement it as well as we can. I will be doing my part, and I expect all of you to do so as well. We'll have another chance to get our oar in next year when the program is evaluated. But in the meantime we have to give it a fair chance and do what we can to make it work.

To ensure that this happens, Burke should ask members of the group, including Mrs. Lowe, what they plan to say to their staff members. This step reasserts the importance of organizational coherence as a value, thus equipping individuals to support the decision in difficult situations (like press interviews or public statements at parents' night). When decision-making processes have been legitimate, middle managers need to carry out the decision and to speak themselves in support of the need for organizational coherence.

12. *Plan how to monitor and support the day-to-day implementation of the decision and communicate these plans to everyone involved.*

Before we leave the decision-making process, we need to make more than a gesture in the direction of implementation. Without attempting here to deliver a tract on implementing plans of action, we would be remiss if we did not acknowledge the need to reserve time on the agendas of regular meetings to review progress toward long-term goals. The best-made decisions and plans are for naught if no one is keeping tabs on the time line and the key action steps. Way back in step 2 we made sure we had adequate resources for carrying out whatever decision might be reached. Now we have to guard against taking on too many new priorities over the coming year so that we don't run out of time to implement the plan we've just made.

Overcoming Factors That Can Impede Even a Good Decision-Making Process

WE'VE ALREADY MENTIONED THE FACT THAT WHAT happens in schools is often dependent on individual personalities and informal communication patterns rather than established procedures. Even with the guidelines, success can be sabotaged unless leaders are aware of some of the subtle—and not so subtle—factors that can affect the course of events: ineffective communication, lack of knowledge about group process, and, simply, the realities of daily life that impinge on our best-made plans. There is much we can do to deal with these potential problems.

Honest, Open Communication

Central to successful decision making is honest and effective communication among participants. This is such an important point that at one time we listed it as a separate guideline. We wanted to highlight its importance, yet we realized that it wasn't a step in a process but a quality that permeates legitimate decision making. And it doesn't happen by accident.

Honest, effective communication, in fact, tends not to happen at all, given human nature and the nature of organizations. People tend not to speak frankly to those in authority. For leaders to overcome this tendency takes special effort and particular skills. Developing such skills and constantly applying them during decision-making processes with groups and individuals is essential. The 12 guidelines both require and reinforce honest, effective communication. The success of the decision-making process will be seriously imperiled, however, unless leaders explicitly call for honest, effective communication from group members, model it in their own daily interactions, and direct group attention to monitor "how we're doing" at it.

Group Process and Facilitation

Of equal importance is having someone who can skillfully facilitate group dynamics within meetings. On the one hand, we want someone with interpersonal communication skills and group-processing knowledge who can make sure essential roles are played (e.g., clarifying, summarizing) and tasks performed (agendas formed, minutes accurately recorded) so that the group functions cohesively and effectively. On the other hand, we want to be sure the group can apply creative thinking strategies to their problem so they come up with good alternatives to consider.

Both of these topics, effective group process and creative generation of alternative solutions, are worth considering separately. In fact, together with legitimate process, the topic of this book, they provide what we believe is a comprehensive syllabus for a course on decision making. Many excellent articles and books are available on these other two topics.[4] Our hope is to provide a missing link in what we believe is now a maturing body of knowledge on decision-making practice, and we urge readers to pursue those other two bodies of literature.

Flexibility in the Face of Reality

It is nice to have a symmetrical list of 12 guidelines to follow, and we do try to follow them as much as possible. But it is also important to understand the asymmetry of real events and point out the ways in which reality may bend a prescriptive list like ours. Our model applies when there are degrees of freedom about whether, how, and how fast to act—in situations involving a problem but not a crisis, when there's a pressure point but not a hemorrhaging wound. It also applies to situations where there isn't a problem or any

---

[4] For example, on group dynamics see M. Doyle and D. Straus' excellent *How to Make Meetings Work* (New York: Jove Press, 1976) and Matthew Miles' *Learning to Work in Groups* (New York: Teachers College Press, 1969). On creative problem solving and generation of alternatives, see S.J. Parnes, *Creative Behavior Guidebook* (New York: Charles Scribner and Sons, 1967); C.E. Wales, A.H. Nardi, and R.A. Stager, *Professional Decision-Making* (Morgantown, W.Va.: Center for Guided Design, 1986); and W.J.J. Gordon, *Synectics* (New York: Harper and Row, 1961).

outside pressure but an individual or group proposes to make an improvement.

Some decisions can skip many of the 12 steps because they are annual or predictable events (e.g., class assignments and scheduling). Other decisions originate in someone's idea for a change or innovation, and all the 12 steps may then be important to consider. The same may be true when responding to a problem. But the more the problem borders on crisis, the faster one needs to act and the more the process may be abbreviated. Even without crisis, however, the nature of the decision may abbreviate the process.

Decision making in most organizations (including schools) spans the three stages of planning, deciding, and implementing, which need to be identified for all constituencies. In stage 1, planning, the decision is whether or not to study an issue (e.g., grade-level reorganization or designing a new social studies curriculum.) The first five steps in our guidelines refer to this planning stage. And the process may go no further because we're able to conclude right away that the issue isn't really worth working on right now. But if it is appropriate to continue, then we do the study. Even then we may find that what we already have is best, or the needed resources turn out to be more than we bargained for, or something else more important has come up.

In the next stage, deciding, we make plans of action and decide which to implement. Again, we still have the option of dropping or temporarily shelving the project. People need to know that we are open to halting the decision-making process at any point if data or priorities so indicate.

Finally, in the implementing stage, we put the plan to work and do what's necessary to enlist and inform those involved, and then monitor the results of our decision.

For issues where there is time, recall that there are several benchmarks where decisions to go ahead are tentative and must be renewed. (This is not true of crises, which by definition can't wait.)

Note also that there is implicit in these 12 steps no statement that consensus decisions are better (because they're not always) or that top-down decisions are better (because they're not always, either). Some decisions should be made and announced swiftly by the boss, and with little consultation. Others definitely need consensus and broad involvement if they are to succeed. In this framework, the whole range of possibilities is allowed as to who will make the decision; it's just that the "who" should be announced clearly, right at the beginning (step 4 above). And the administrator responsible (step 3) should look carefully at whom the issue affects most and who needs to buy in if the decision is to be carried out well.

Uses of the Decision-Making Guidelines

WE ADVOCATE MAKING THE GUIDELINES PUBLIC within an organization. Consistent with this is our position that anyone should be able to propose an issue for discussion and decision from any level in the organization. That is necessary if we are to work toward the goal of having everyone be a responsible decision maker. At this point, let's consider how the guidelines can serve these and other goals.

Strengthening School Culture

Having *everyone a responsible decision maker* is a goal connected to building a strong school culture. Our advocacy of this goal proceeds from a belief that successful organizations promote responsible participation by all their members; that is, they enlist the energies and ideas of many members and generate commitment throughout the organization for its policies.

Once again, we are not saying all decisions can or should be reached through democratic participation (though some should be). We are calling for responsible involvement from everyone. This commitment develops only if there is widespread acceptance of the decision-making process. Acceptance does not mean members agree with every decision, but it does mean they respect and feel respected by the process that arrived at it. (See especially step 11, closing the loop.)

Beyond acceptance, however, we want people to be actively involved, for several reasons. One is that the more people who participate, the more ideas will be generated and the better the decision is likely to be. Second, the more people participate, the more the information, the rationale, and the intentions behind the decision get communicated—and the better the implementation will be. Both of these reasons, important as they may be, are less important than the third. This third reason really defines *active participants*.

Everyone a responsible decision maker is an organizational value that says, "Around here, people speak up about what they think we should do, and they think about the interests of the whole school, not just their own sphere. We encourage all our people from all levels to initiate ideas and discuss issues that are important to them. We don't expect everyone to care about or get involved in every decision. But when they choose to do so, we respect and reward them for acting that way, even if we don't wind up doing what they suggest."

A school organization that realizes this value gets the best from its people and will be constantly improving. Our 12 guidelines for decision making are directly linked to this value. Thus, one of the uses of this decision-making model is to energize the people in the school across the board. We can expect that this energy will also be more focused on common goals that will emerge from this kind of decision making.

Monitoring Decisions in Progress

Decision makers can keep the guidelines (or a subset of the guidelines that they have identified as particularly important) posted on the wall (literally or figuratively) and use them to monitor their progress—checkpoints, as it were—for a good process. Chronologically, the guidelines can be introduced at any point in a decision-making process. One possibility would be to do so early on, while a group is exploring a policy issue, then to reintroduce the framework if and when the group determines that an existing policy needs to be changed or that a new one needs to be introduced. Another use would be to bring up the framework before arriving at a conclusion so that group members can assure themselves that the process was satisfactory. In doing so they may learn ways of improving their next decision.

Retrospective Analysis

The guidelines provide a common language to enable a group to analyze its decision-making strengths and weaknesses. For example, a management team or a faculty

might review some of its past decisions at the
end of a year in an effort to identify and
replicate good decision-making practices.
Building administrators might do the same,
both on their own and in discussion with
faculty members. The more that individuals
and groups engage in this kind of activity, the
more they should learn about their decision-
making patterns and biases. The resulting
learning should lead to better decisions.

The guidelines thus have both prospective
and retrospective uses. When used over a
period of time, they should enable
administrators and decision-making groups to
analyze and monitor their own actions. Most
important, they should increase the chances
that all members of a school community will
take the initiative in making and contributing
to responsible, informed choices concerning
the life of the community.

Conclusion

To Some, These 12 Steps May Seem To Offer little that is new. To this we would respond in several ways. First, we believe that most administrators and decision-making groups carry out some of these steps but that few act on them all with consistency. Second, we think it is possible for decision makers to believe they are acting according to such principles but remain unaware of ways in which they are not. This can happen easily since most discussions about decisions are about their content; *how* a decision will be made is rarely discussed in public, or even in private. As a result, decision makers can lack understanding of their own blind spots. The same is true of classroom teachers. For teachers, we devise supervisory systems to help them learn about and compensate for blind spots. We believe administrators and decision-making groups could also benefit from similar analyses of their decision-making performance, but that new ways need to be devised for them to gather data on their performance. We hope that these guidelines will provide one such method.

On the other hand, we recognize that there are potential barriers to overcome in implementing guidelines like ours. One possible objection is that they are too elaborate: decision makers might view our suggestions as difficult to use because they would be too time consuming. One way to deal with this reservation is to isolate and work only with the three or four guidelines the faculty needs to focus on most.

In order to use the 12 guidelines, decision makers will need to make an investment of time, an already scarce commodity. Obviously, we believe the investment is worth it, since the return will be improved efficiency, effectiveness, and morale. In addition, the initial cost in time diminishes as people become accustomed to using the guidelines and adapt them to their own particular circumstances. Finally, it may be that a shortage of time points to problems with the condition of life in schools as much as it demonstrates the difficulties of implementing these guidelines.

Some leaders may not wish to use the guidelines to solicit feedback on their decision-making process. There is little precedent for school administrators to elicit feedback about their management of decision making, and even less for members of decision-making groups to critique their own performance. We see two main reasons for this. First, we have yet to develop a language for these processes; our guidelines are intended as a first step toward developing one. Second, administrators are expected to "know" how to lead groups in making decisions. While principals are not expected to know everything about the substance of every decision, it might be seen as a sign of weakness if they appear not to know how to evaluate choices, influence faculty members, and build consensus. This is an incomplete and unfortunate view of leadership. In our view, it is a sign of strength for leaders and management groups to openly examine the ways in which they make decisions. Not only can examination lead to better decisions, it is also a means of creating more responsive and responsible forms of school governance.

Finally, we recognize that it is easier to recommend honest, open communication than to practice it. This is a vital ingredient of our guidelines, one that informs the other aspects in many ways. It is also an area in which all of us have some blind spots. We hope that those who try the guidelines will recognize this possible difficulty and keep it in mind when they reflect on their own and others' performance.

References

Darling-Hammond, L. (August 4, 1987). "Who Should Be Schools' Instructional Leaders?" *Education Week,* p.44.

Rallis, S.F., and M.C. Highsmith. (December 1986). "The Myth of the Great Principal." *Phi Delta Kappan,* pp. 300-304.

Saphier, J.D., and M. King. (March 1985). "Good Seeds Grow in Strong Cultures." *Educational Leadership* 42:67 - 74.

About the Authors

JON SAPHIER is an experienced elementary and secondary level supervisor and classroom teacher, former staff developer for the Cambridge Public Schools, and instructor at Boston University. The author of *The Skillful Teacher,* Saphier is currently president of Research for Better Teaching in Carlisle, Massachusetts, and a consultant on supervision, evaluation, and staff development.

TOM BIGDA-PEYTON, also of the Boston area, has served as history/social studies teacher in grades 7–12 and middle school and high school principal. He currently provides consulting and inservice training on collaborative approaches to negotiation and conflict management and conducts team-building workshops for decision-making groups such as superintendents and school boards.

GEOFF PIERSON has worked in the Boston area as teacher, department head, and area coordinator, and for the Lexington, Massachusetts, public schools as assistant superintendent for instruction and, later, superintendent. He is currently director of the American International School in Vienna, Austria.